The POWER of POSITIVE DRINKING

Coloring Book

galison
www.galison.com f🅞 @galisongift
70 West 36th Street, 11th Floor
New York, NY 10018

Images used under license from Shutterstock.com

ISBN: 978-0-7353-6710-4

First Edition: 2020

Designed and printed in the United States of America.

10 9 8 7 6 5 4 3 2

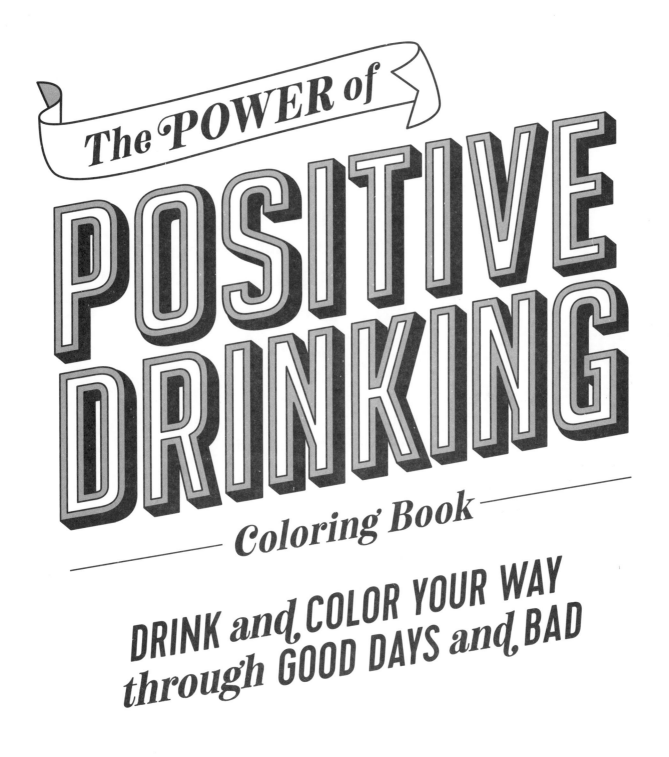

The POWER of

POSITIVE DRINKING

Coloring Book

DRINK and COLOR YOUR WAY through GOOD DAYS and BAD

Hemingway DAIQUIRI

Named after a literary icon who knew his liquor as well as his words, the Hemingway Daiquiri is a sweet and zesty refresher. If you prefer your daiquiris frozen, mix the ingredients in a blender with ice. Just make sure to drink it while reading a good book.

2 oz white rum
¼ oz maraschino liqueur
¾ oz grapefruit juice
½ oz lime juice
¼ oz simple syrup

In a cocktail shaker filled with ice, combine the ingredients.
Shake and strain into a cocktail glass and enjoy.

I drink to make other people MORE INTERESTING.

—ERNEST HEMINGWAY

Whole Lotta COLADA

Put a spring in your step with the Whole Lotta Colada.
No frills here—stir up a traditional piña colada without the hassle of a blender
and all the bliss of pineapple and coconut. (But blend away, if you wish!) Sip
this in paradise or make paradise come to you with every tip of the glass.

2 oz light rum
3 oz pineapple juice
1 ½ oz cream of coconut
1 pineapple slice
1 maraschino cherry

In a cocktail glass filled with ice, combine the ingredients and enjoy.

Here's to alcohol: the cause of and
SOLUTION TO ALL LIFE'S PROBLEMS.

—HOMER SIMPSON

Strawberry-Mint MOJITO

Strawberry and mint, mint and strawberry—such a wonderful pair that deserves a special place in a cocktail glass. While a traditional mojito is downright lovely, the fresh strawberries are the key to this cocktail and add just the right amount of fruity sweetness.

3–4 fresh strawberries
2–3 mint leaves
1 oz simple syrup
1 oz lime juice
2 oz light rum
3 oz club soda

In a highball glass, muddle strawberries, mint, and simple syrup. Stir in the lime juice and rum. Fill the glass with ice, top with club soda, and enjoy.

THERE CANNOT BE GOOD LIVING
where there is no good drinking.
—BENJAMIN FRANKLIN

Easy-Breezy
PEACH BELLINI

This drink is the nectar of the gods. You can purchase peach purée at the store or blend it up at home. If you don't have prosecco, champagne or cava will do the trick. Sip this sweet ambrosia and make your dreams come true.

5 oz prosecco
1 oz peach purée
1-2 mint leaves

Pour prosecco into a champagne flute and add the peach purée. Garnish with mint and enjoy.

HERE'S TO ALCOHOL,
the rose-colored glasses of life.

—F. SCOTT FITZGERALD

Mint JULEP

On a refreshing summer day or when you're just feeling fresh, drink down a Mint Julep. The coolness of the crushed ice and the aromatic mint make this bourbon libation an easy-drinking pick-me-up for any occasion.

4 mint leaves
1 teaspoon sugar
1 splash water
3 oz bourbon whiskey

In a highball glass, gently muddle the mint, sugar, and water. Fill the glass with crushed ice, add the bourbon, and stir. Garnish with a mint sprig and enjoy.

THERE IS NO BAD WHISKEY.
There are only some whiskeys that aren't as good as others.

—RAYMOND CHANDLER

Colorado COOLER

Step aside, maraschino cherries. The Colorado Cooler is a delightful blend of whiskey, citrus, and stone fruit. Fresh cherries prevent this drink from getting too sweet so you can enjoy a mighty, yet drinkable whiskey cocktail.

5 fresh cherries
2 oz whiskey
1 oz club soda
¾ oz lemon juice
¾ oz simple syrup

Pit four of the cherries. In a cocktail shaker, muddle the pitted cherries. Add ice, and combine the whiskey, club soda, lemon juice, and simple syrup. Shake and strain into a highball glass with ice. Garnish with the last cherry and enjoy.

ACCORDING TO SCIENCE,
alcohol is a solution.

Prosecco and
ELDERFLOWER COCKTAIL

Add a little oomph to your champagne flute with the Prosecco & Elderflower Cocktail. Sweet without being too sugary, the floral notes of the liqueur and the chill of the cucumber make this an extra-refreshing offering.

1 oz elderflower liqueur
4 oz prosecco, chilled
2-3 slices cucumber

In a champagne flute, add the elderflower liqueur, and then fill the rest of the glass with prosecco. Garnish with the cucumber slices and enjoy.

❋

There comes a time in every woman's life
WHEN THE ONLY THING THAT HELPS
is a glass of champagne.

—BETTE DAVIS

Fernet con COLA

Two-ingredient cocktails are the best kind of cocktails. Fernet is an aromatic spirit that tastes a bit like black licorice, and this Argentine-born cocktail is a wonder in a glass. The blend of bitter and sweet in Fernet con Cola makes this a reviving and refreshing drink.

2 oz cola
1 oz Fernet-Branca
1 lemon twist

In a highball glass filled with ice, combine the Fernet and cola. Garnish with a lemon twist and enjoy.

I WOULD RATHER HAVE A FREE BOTTLE
in front of me than a pre-frontal lobotomy.

—DEAN MARTIN

Maple-Bourbon MOJO

Raise a glass of liquid confidence with the Maple-Bourbon Mojo. In another life, this drink would be reminiscent of an Old Fashioned, but a drizzle of maple gives it a new soul entirely. Boost your confidence while you boost your bourbon intake with every clink of the glass.

½ oz maple syrup
½ oz orange juice
½ oz lemon juice
1 orange wheel
2 oz bourbon
Splash club soda

In a cocktail glass, combine the maple syrup, orange juice, and lemon juice. Lightly muddle the orange wheel. Add the bourbon and fill the glass with ice. Top with club soda and enjoy.

THAT'S WHAT I LIKE TO DO:
I drink and I know things!

—TYRION LANNISTER

Caipirinha

A traditional Brazilian beverage that tastes like summer and drinks like water, the Caipirinha is sure to add a spring in your step after just a few sips. Refreshing, tart, and sweet all at once, it's the perfect drink if you're by the beach or just wish you were.

½ lime, quartered
½ tsp sugar
2 oz cachaça

In a cocktail glass, muddle the lime and the sugar. Fill the glass with ice, add the cachaça, and enjoy.

A BOTTLE OF WINE CONTAINS MORE philosophy than all the books in the world.

—LOUIS PASTEUR

Elderflower PICK-ME-UP

Some cocktails are made to inspire happiness. The Elderflower Pick-Me-Up is just that drink, with floral notes and refreshing cucumber to round it all out. Stir this up and make a toast to happiness.

2 oz gin
1 oz elderflower liqueur
Splash prosecco
4 cucumber slices

In a high ball glass filled with ice, combine the gin and the elderflower liqueur. Pour a splash of prosecco, garnish with cucumber, and enjoy.

I believe in the power
OF POSITIVE DRINKING.

Tom COLLINS

Boost your spirits with a Tom Collins! A dose of gin, a splash of lemon, and a spritz of fizz, this classic cocktail needs no modifications or fancy updates. Sip it down any time of year for a cooling blend of gin and citrus.

2 oz dry gin
1 oz lemon juice
½ oz simple syrup
3½ oz club soda
1 lemon twist

In a highball glass filled with ice, combine the gin, lemon juice, simple syrup, and club soda. Garnish with the lemon twist and enjoy.

Keep your gin up!

I'm Not Even
DRUNK DAIQUIRI

Cucumber makes everything taste cool and light, and this daiquiri is no exception. A crisp twist on the classic rum drink, the I'm Not Even Drunk Daiquiri is the cocktail equivalent to stepping into a refreshing island waterfall. Taste your way into a tipsier day with one pleasant libation.

4–6 cucumber slices
¾ oz lime juice
½ oz simple syrup
1 ½ oz light rum
1 cucumber twist

In a cocktail shaker filled with ice, combine the ingredients. Shake and strain into a coupe glass. Garnish with the cucumber twist and enjoy.

Alcohol is the anesthesia by which
WE ENDURE THE OPERATION OF LIFE.

—GEORGE BERNARD SHAW

Michelada

Cool, spicy, and refreshing, the Michelada is the best flavors of summer in one cocktail glass. The tart citrus, and big, bold flavors of the sauces create a flavor-packed base. With a pour of an easy-drinking beer, those flavors smooth out for one truly satisfying drink.

1½ oz lime juice

2 tsp hot sauce

1 tsp Worcestershire sauce

1 pinch of salt

1 (12-oz) Mexican beer

1 tbsp chili salt

Line the dampened rim of a pint glass with the chili salt. Combine the lime juice, hot sauce, Worcestershire sauce, and pinch of salt in the glass. Fill the glass with ice and then pour the beer at an angle until the glass is full, and enjoy.

My doctor told me to watch my drinking.
NOW I DRINK IN FRONT OF A MIRROR.

—RODNEY DANGERFIELD

Son of a SPRITZ

Toil away the rosé way with the Son of a Spritz. This blend of bubbles and berries is the peppy addition to the spritz family. A mix of rosé cider and elderflower, it's refreshing without being too sweet. Nurse it or crush it, but definitely let it brighten your day.

4 oz dry rosé cider
1 oz elderflower liqueur
Splash club soda
2–4 torn mint leaves
Handful of blueberries

In a cocktail glass filled with ice, combine the ingredients and enjoy.

Ho! Ho! Ho! To the bottle I go.
TO HEAL MY HEART AND DROWN MY WOE...

—J.R.R. TOLKIEN

Classic Martini
ON THE ROCKS

A classic for a reason, the gin martini is the epitome of style. This no-nonsense drink embraces botanical bite of gin, with a spritz of citrus for some flair. After one, you'll be singing its praises; after two, those of everyone around you.

3 oz London dry-style gin
¾ oz dry vermouth
1 lemon twist

In a mixing glass filled with ice, add the gin and vermouth and stir for 30 seconds. Strain the liquid into a rocks glass filled with fresh ice. Garnish with the lemon twist and enjoy.

I EXERCISE SELF-CONTROL AND NEVER TOUCH
a beverage stronger than gin before breakfast.

—W.C. FIELDS

Jalapeño MARGARITA

Fire meets ice with the Jalapeño Margarita. With the zest of lime, the smoothness of agave, the heat of jalapeño, and the inhibition of tequila, this drink has it all.

3-4 slices jalapeño
½ oz agave syrup
3 oz silver tequila
1 oz fresh lime juice
1 wedge lime

In a cocktail shaker, muddle 2 jalapeño slices and the agave syrup. Add the tequila and lime juice, and fill with ice. Shake and strain into a cocktail glass. Garnish with the remaining jalapeños and the lime wedge and enjoy.

FIRST YOU TAKE A DRINK,
then the drink takes a drink,
THEN THE DRINK TAKES YOU.

—F. SCOTT FITZGERALD

Sidecar

A drink that has never gone out of style, the classic Sidecar is a cocktail lover's dream. A perfect arrangement of brandy, orange liqueur, and lemon juice, this no-nonsense cocktail is potent, citrusy, and altogether warming.

1½ oz Cognac

1 oz Cointreau

½ oz lemon juice

2 tbsp sugar

1 lemon twist

Line the dampened rim of a coupe glass with sugar. In a cocktail shaker filled with ice, combine the Cognac, Cointreau, and lemon juice. Shake and strain into the glass. Garnish with the lemon twist and enjoy.

Reality is an illusion
CREATED BY A LACK OF ALCOHOL.

—N.F. SIMPSON

Summer SHANDY

Pour some sunshine into your glass! This mix of beer and lemonade is one of the most refreshing drinks you'll ever try. Choose an easy-drinking beer that won't overpower the lemonade, such as a pilsner or a light lager.

1 bottle light beer
6 oz cold lemonade
1 lemon slice

Fill a pint glass two-thirds of the way with beer and then add lemonade. Garnish with lemon and enjoy.

I WORK UNTIL BEER O'CLOCK.

—STEPHEN KING

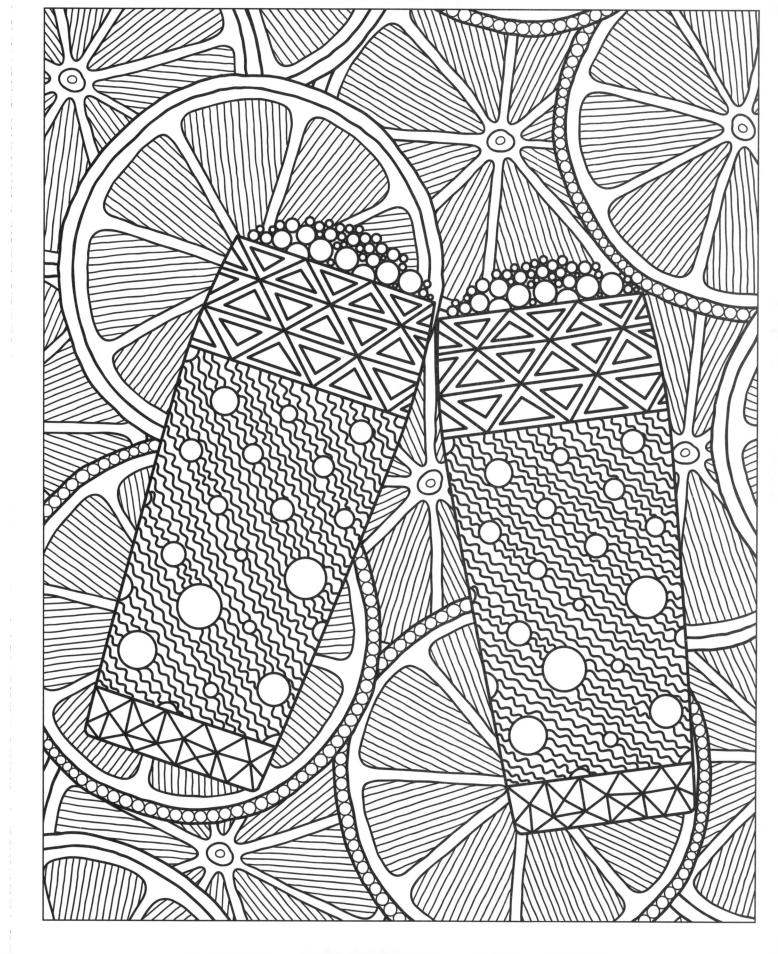

Make Your Point
MARGARITA

One tequila, two tequila, three tequila, floor—drink up with this cactus-inspired margarita. Prickly pear purée makes for a bright fuchsia cocktail that's as pretty as it is fun to drink. With a subtle melon-meets-bubblegum flavor, it will make you forget that it was born of the desert's meanest plant.

1 ½ oz silver tequila
1 oz prickly pear purée
¾ oz agave syrup
¾ oz lime juice
1 lemon twist

In a cocktail shaker filled with ice, combine the tequila, prickly pear purée, agave syrup, and lime juice. Shake and strain into a coupe glass. Garnish with the twist and enjoy.

You're not drunk if you can lie on
THE FLOOR WITHOUT HOLDING ON.

—DEAN MARTIN

Screw-It SCREWDRIVER

Shake up your screwdriver game with a little something extra. The cinnamon-sugar rim adds sweetness and spice to this faithful cocktail, making it perfect for autumn afternoons or brunch ballyhoo alike. If you're in it for the show, skip the rim and go for a torched cinnamon stick instead.

2 tbsp cinnamon sugar

1 ½ oz vodka

3 oz fresh orange juice

1 orange slice

Line the dampened rim of a cocktail class with the cinnamon sugar. Fill the glass with ice and add the vodka and orange juice. Garnish with the orange slice and enjoy.

I DISTRUST CAMELS, AND ANYONE
else who can go a week without a drink.

—JOE E. LEWIS

Escape to PARADISE

When a tropical vacation is out of reach, make one in a glass. Smoothly sweet with a bit of citrus, Escape to Paradise is the cocktail version of a beachside sunset. Sip it down and raise a glass to relaxation!

1 oz vodka
½ oz Chambord
3 oz sweet and sour mix
Juice from 1 lemon wedge
Dash grenadine

In a cocktail glass filled with ice, combine the ingredients and enjoy.

TRUST ME, YOU CAN DANCE.

—VODKA

Bubble TROUBLE

The love-child of a mimosa and a spritz, this perky drink is made for Sunday Fundays and long brunches. The orange bitters mellow out the grapefruit while adding a touch of color. Tear the mint leaves for added aroma.

4 oz prosecco
1 oz grapefruit juice
1 oz club soda
3-4 dashes orange bitters
2 torn mint leaves

In a wine glass filled with ice, combine the ingredients and enjoy.

WINE IS SUNLIGHT,
held together by water.

—GALILEO

Mint Espresso MARTINI

When caffeine just isn't working, combine that caffeine with booze. Perfect for a cold winter night or as a sumptuous dessert, the Mint Espresso Martini will add that extra spring in your step just when you need it.

1 oz mint-chocolate Irish cream
2 oz espresso vodka
1 mint sprig

In a cocktail shaker filled with ice, combine the Irish cream and the espresso vodka. Shake and strain into a cocktail glass, garnish with mint, and enjoy.

STEP ASIDE, COFFEE.
This is a job for alcohol.

Summer WINE-NOT

A take on the Spanish wine cocktail, tinto de verano, this beauty is the perfect excuse to guzzle red wine on a hot day. An easy mix of table wine and lemonade, you can stir up this lazy-man's sangria in no time.

4 oz dry red wine
2 oz lemonade
1–2 orange slices

In a cocktail glass filled with ice, combine the ingredients and enjoy.

WHAT CONTEMPTIBLE SCOUNDREL
has stolen the cork to my lunch?

—W.C. FIELDS

La Marseillaise

A sweet and citrusy treat, La Marseillaise will take you away to a lakeside chalet in France. If your imagination doesn't take you farther away than your own kitchen table—have two.

1½ oz citrus vodka
¾ oz peach Schnapps
Juice of ½ lemon
Dash cranberry juice cocktail
1 orange twist

In a cocktail shaker filled with ice, combine the vodka, peach Schnapps, lemon juice, and cranberry juice. Shake and strain into a coupe glass. Garnish with the orange twist and enjoy.

THE PROBLEM WITH THE WORLD IS THAT
everyone is a few drinks behind.

—HUMPHREY BOGART

Vanilla-Pumpkin
BOILERMAKER

Boilermakers of yore were beer and a shot of bourbon. This younger, spunkier version just got all dressed up in pumpkin spice and isn't afraid to show it. Best enjoyed during crisp autumn weather, you can take your time savoring this one.

1 oz vanilla vodka
1 bottle pumpkin beer
1 tbsp agave
2 tbsp cinnamon sugar

Line the rim of a pint glass with the agave and cinnamon sugar. Pour the vodka into the glass, and then pour the beer at an angle until the glass is full. Enjoy.

ONE KIND WORD CAN
change someone's day: vodka.

Ginger-Ale SIPPER

Ginger beer lovers, unite! A combination of wheat beer, ginger beer, lemon, and rosemary—this drink is fit for a lazy afternoon or a stroll in the park. If you don't have rosemary, garnish with another herb or aromatic like thyme, mint, or basil.

1 bottle cold Belgian-style wheat beer
6 oz cold ginger beer
1 rosemary sprig

Fill a pint glass two-thirds of the way with beer and then add ginger beer. Garnish with rosemary and enjoy.

Everybody's got to believe in something
I BELIEVE I'LL HAVE ANOTHER BEER.

—W.C. FIELDS

Negroni

Drink to your health with a sip or several of a Negroni. This classic cocktail brings a blend of bitter, sweet, and zesty orange to your evening. Drink before dinner if you're a purist, drink any time if you're not.

1 oz dry gin
1 oz Campari
1 oz sweet vermouth
1 orange twist

In a cocktail glass filled with ice, combine the gin, Campari, and sweet vermouth. Garnish with the orange twist and enjoy.

ALCOHOL: BECAUSE NO GREAT STORY EVER
started with someone eating a salad.

Corpse Reviver NO. 2

First imagined as a hangover cure in the late 19th century, the Corpse Reviver No. 2 is a classic gin cocktail that stands the test of time. The absinthe wash and dose of citrus are enough to perk any one up, but this hair of the dog is as delightful as it is reviving.

1 splash Absinthe
¾ oz gin
¾ oz Lillet Blanc
¾ oz Cointreau
¾ oz lemon juice
1 orange twist

Rinse a coupe glass with absinthe. In a cocktail shaker filled with ice, combine the gin, Lillet Blanc, Cointreau, and lemon juice. Shake and strain into the glass. Garnish with the orange twist and enjoy.

When I read about the evils OF DRINKING, I GAVE UP READING.

—HENNY YOUNGMAN

Rosé SANGRIA

A fresh take on a classic, Rosé Sangria has all the elements of traditional red sangria with a playfully pink spin. The ginger adds just a little bit of a zing, and the basil complements the strawberry. Perfect for a patio or a picnic, or maybe just a more joyful Tuesday.

4 oz dry rosé

½ oz ginger liqueur

Splash of prosecco

1 strawberry, destemmed and sliced

4 cucumber slices

2 torn basil leaves

In a wine glass filled with ice, combine the ingredients and enjoy.

———————————————— ❀ ————————————————

It's wine o'clock somewhere.

Put Your Mojito
WHERE YOUR MOUTH IS

Watch out for this easy-drinker. Thirst-quenching and delicious, the cucumbers and basil are an unlikely twist to the traditional mojito. Drink one to savor a mojito moment, drink more to make promises you might just have to keep.

2 oz light rum

1 oz lime juice

½ oz simple syrup

2–4 torn basil leaves

4–6 sliced cucumbers

Splash club soda

In a cocktail glass filled with ice, combine the ingredients and enjoy.

ALWAYS DO SOBER WHAT YOU SAID
you'd do drunk. That will teach you
TO KEEP YOUR MOUTH SHUT.

—ERNEST HEMINGWAY

Aperol SPRITZ

An Aperol Spritz is the easy-drinking delight that's the adult equivalent of running through a sprinkler. Refreshing, pleasant, and altogether memorable, this simple and forgiving cocktail will be your sunny day and your party go-to.

4 oz prosecco
2 oz Aperol
Splash club soda
1 orange twist

In a wine glass filled with ice, combine the prosecco and Aperol, and finish with a splash of club soda. Garnish with an orange twist and enjoy.

Drink happy thoughts!

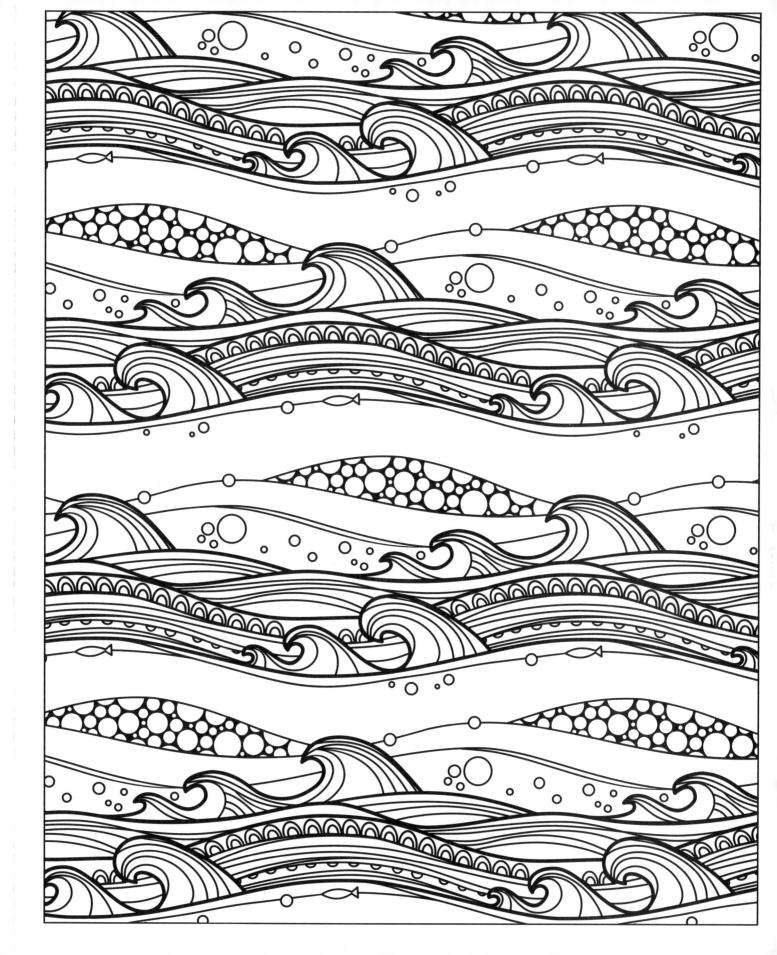

Classic MANHATTAN

Powerful and refined—just like the city it's named for—there is nothing quite like a Classic Manhattan. If you're easing your way into whiskey drinking, add a splash of syrup from the cherry jar to sweeten it up.

2 oz rye whiskey
1 oz sweet vermouth
Dash Angostura bitters
1 maraschino cherry

In a mixing glass filled with ice, stir the whiskey, vermouth, and bitters. Strain the liquid into a cocktail glass. Garnish with a cherry and enjoy.

Whiskey is liquid sunshine.

—GEORGE BERNARD SHAW

Dark and STORMY

Batten down the hatches and prepare for the Dark and Stormy. An old standby that has weathered many seasons of cocktail trends, it's a drink that's easy to make and will quench any thirst.

2 oz dark rum
5 oz ginger beer
1 lime wedge

In a highball glass filled with ice, combine the dark rum and ginger beer. Garnish with the lime wedge and enjoy.

IN WINE THERE IS WISDOM, IN BEER
there is freedom, in water there is bacteria.

Pick-a-Pepper PALOMA

Some like it hot with this spicy take on a Paloma cocktail. Muddle the jalapeño slices to get the most heat, or leave them be and nurse this drink for a slow and steady burn. Enjoy the zip of the grapefruit and the chill of the ice as you savor the Pick-a-Pepper Paloma.

1 ½ oz tequila
½ oz lime juice
4 ½ oz grapefruit soda
2–4 jalapeño slices

In a cocktail glass filled with ice, combine the ingredients and enjoy.

Always remember that I have TAKEN MORE OUT OF ALCOHOL THAN alcohol has taken out of me.

—WINSTON CHURCHILL

Bee's KNEES

A cocktail that dreams are made of, the Bee's Knees is a delightful blend of citrus, honey, and booze that makes everything a little bit brighter. If you don't have honey simple syrup, substitute a drop or two of regular honey instead.

2 oz gin
¾ oz lemon juice
¾ oz honey simple syrup
1 lemon twist

In a cocktail glass filled with ice, combine the gin, lemon juice, and simple syrup. Garnish with the lemon twist and enjoy.

Alcohol may be man's worst enemy, BUT THE BIBLE SAYS LOVE YOUR ENEMY.

—FRANK SINATRA

Pisco POWER HOUR

You can't have sweet without a little sour, and the Pisco Power Hour is a great place to start. The egg white gives this traditional Peruvian cocktail a smooth, easy-drinking effervescence that goes down best on a sunny day. Drink to a healthy pour in every glass and happiness in every sip.

1 ½ oz pisco
1 oz lemon juice
¾ oz simple syrup
1 egg white
2 dashes Angostura bitters
1 lime wheel

In a cocktail shaker filled with ice, combine the pisco, lemon juice, simple syrup, and egg white. Shake vigorously and strain into a coupe glass. Add the bitters, garnish with a lime wheel, and enjoy.

Why limit happy TO AN HOUR?